LIFTING
THE STONE

Poems
by
JASON
SOMMER

FOREST
BOOKS
London & Boston

PUBLISHED BY
FOREST BOOKS

20 Forest View, Chingford, London E4 7 AY, U.K.
P.O. Box 438, Wayland, MA 01778, U.S.A.

First Published 1991

Typeset in the United States
by Poole, Johnson & Co.
Printed in Great Britain by BPCC Wheatons Ltd, Exeter

Poems copyright Jason Sommer
Cover art by Pat Schuchard
Photograph by Richard Hinners

British Library Cataloging in Publication Data

Sommer, Jason
Lifting The Stone: poems
I. Title   II. Sommer, Jason
811.54

ISBN 0–948259–94–9

Library of Congress Catalog Card Number
90–84193

FOREST BOOKS

LIFTING THE STONE

JASON SOMMER was born in the Bronx in 1950. He received his B.A. from Brandeis University, his M.A. from Stanford, where he held the Mirrielees Fellowship in Poetry, and his Ph.D. from Saint Louis University. His poems have appeared in many magazines, including *The New Republic, Ploughshares, Occident, Chicago Review,* and *The Honest Ulsterman.* Resident in Ireland from 1974 to 1981, he taught at University College Dublin, and reviewed for the *Irish Independent.* His English versions of contemporary Irish language poems have appeared in *International Poetry Review, Innti* magazine's translation supplement, *Selected Poems/Rogha Danta* 1968-1984 by Michael Davitt, and most recently in *Portrait of the Artist as an Abominable Snowman* by Gabriel Rosenstock. Among the awards he has won for his poetry are *The Lyric* magazine's "New England Prize," and an Anna Davidson Rosenberg Award for poems on the Jewish Experience. He teaches literature and creative writing at Fontbonne College in St. Louis, Missouri.

For my parents, for Bernardine, for Matthias, Danielle, and Benjamin.

Jason Sommer

Manuscript

Those ten years, and these few poems,
and getting fewer all the time—
for even now I winnow them,
and end in discarding. Certain rhymes

are as past revising as the events,
the people mostly, they depict.
It feels a kind of permanence
revoked, though, that the five or six

about her come to four, then three;
that one remains of him, diminished
by eight lines. And what can it mean—
what isn't there, not just unfinished,

also untried in poems? Either,
what ever way you reckon it,
poetry's not how worth is measured—
or something like the opposite:

know by all of this—proportion
and attrition—experience, well-rated
in poetry, ten years or more,
is not in poems compensated.

Contents

Acknowledgements

My grateful acknowledgements go to the editors of the following publications in which some of the poems appeared:

Chicago Review, Cutting Edge Quarterly, Delmar, Literature and Belief, Mosaic, New CollAge, Occident, Ploughshares, Reconstructionist, Response Magazine, River Styx, The Honest Ulsterman, The Lyric, The New Republic, The Webster Reveiw

With special thanks to Richard Moran for all his support: the reading and comment, and ordering of the poems.

This book was published with the assistance of a faculty development grant from Fontbonne College, Clayton, Missouri.

LIFTING THE STONE

Amnesia

Wakening late, and light blazed yellow
through curtains and down the pine floor-boards
which led from the window to the rush-bottom chair

beside the bed—not a Van Gogh yellow
for I had no Van Gogh anywhere in mind
nor even *yellow*. The lips formed

by the creases in the sheet were not lips, creases,
or sheet. Each thing surveyed nothing
like anything else, yet everything itself,

exactly, though I had no idea of words.
The stained-glass light blinked several times
blinded by a rising or setting bird

as I can say now but would have been just then
unable to say, calmly unable even
to recover my name or make the room my room

or the body in the bed me, infant, Adam,
clown, anyone who by definition
did not know the use of anything

and might bring sheet to mouth or paw at dust-motes.
As it happened, I only looked, my whole face
feeling as if it were an open eye.

For some minutes, whosoever I was was
breathing in the original light of wakening,
from the belly like a singer: in, quick

as delight, and out—a slow stream which tumbled
from sibilance to something like speech,
and when I knew I had laughed, and thought of it

as the call of a late-dreamer under a sun
high enough to reach over garden trees,
no answer to anything else in creation he'd name,

not the pluck of a nerve, but there in the voice
as a kind of proof that beneath sad facts to come
to say in time was a laugh like a given note

of the earliest music of the animal
who speaks and will remember—I, by then, had
of course already long returned to myself.

David

In Somerville, Mass., "All American City"
(title holder nineteen seventy-two)
tonight it is Palestine in the doldrums
within *hamsin* when air baked in a desert
settles in town, sits square in rooms, oblong
in the corridors, presses flat against the sides
of our houses, penned in the alleys between,
so even the curtains hold their feathery breath
in the windows, and night is a room crowded
with the feverish---sweat like sudden tears starts
at the least motion.
                    Nevertheless, I wander
my apartment till, across the way, below
a little, illumined by the yellow moon
of a bulb, a woman turns in her shower slowly,
hooked on a line of sight, in a silver-bead
curtain of water, flat streams of dark hair
and pursed lips as she figureheads into the spray,
then arching down to tend one ankle,
her back breaks the water, her droplet breasts
lead rivulets from their tips, and her hands flow
all over in the veils of water as she performs
her privacy for me.
                    I keep as still
as hunter and quarry both, for sound travels
in the heat as over water. Desire that surged
now goes to ground in a heat that pushes lust
beyond enactment, into mind.
                    Had I
come upon her husband in that window or
another, delaying then to observe the oddity
of my nakedness confirmed as human, seen
in him, what acts might he make natural
for me?
                    I may look in on him as he
looks in on someone else, on anyone

4

but me, or in a book, and reads aloud
gesturing strangely—or does, alone or not,
what I would do. Or wouldn't. What can he
hold back, not knowing we're here?
                                    To look unobserved
into another life and make other lives
grandiose persistence of old story:
Later, when it cools a little, bring her
to me; send him to where the fighting is.

Samson to the Philistines

At first it was like a beautiful dream, dreamt
by a bookish people during a long defeat
to show what a dedicated, a consecrated
man could do.
                        I moved among you freely
as an insult to an entire people moves
among and through them if they even half
believe it.
                        I had a tongue as swift as a brace
of blazing foxtails, vixen and dog bound
together, burning down your blond corn.
But all I had to say to you might be said
with the jawbone of an ass: the vowel-less words
of blows striking, the all-vowel cry
of the stricken.
                        Yet I kept to forms of words
I said heroically, even if you cheated.
Making good on them was honor, a running
bet I made with myself with myself as stakes.

I put up thirty suits of clothes and paid
up thirty suits of clothes I emptied of
your men.
                        My acts rhetorical in the extreme
parallel phrases in reply but always
hyperbolic.
                        You waited ambush all night
by Gaza City's gates. By morning—gates
and post and all I'd carried neatly off
into the hills.
                        Not surprising once
you got the drift and listened hard for what
I might say, what let slip. For what I said
I'd do I'd do as sole interpreter
of what I said. Actions followed words.

6

Riddles came from what happened—
                              out of the eater
food—and everything seemed to be in them:
words and their antonyms, images and their obverse,
deeds and their undoing;
                    strength from sweetness,
the vengeful sweetness of a final strength—
first, honeycombs inside a lion's carcass;
lastly, the carcasses in the honeycombed rubble
of the great hall, thousands blind in their sockets
lidded by the fallen roof.
                         And answer
me these: why should I have told you anything,
especially my secrets?
                      How is it that
the darkness at the story's close, which is
the story's close and also death, derived
from my susceptibility to loving you?

Onan

How goodly are thy tents O Israel
and good the spaces in between,
guy-lined and pegged interstices
of tribe, and further off, the margins
between ourselves and all the rest
where we toss out what we don't want:
the shucked skin of fruit, the pits within,
parts of the animal unwanted
or unclean. I snake around these places
a temptation to myself alone.
The wife does not misunderstand.
She knows I won't come in to her,
beloved brother's hated Tamar,
my hated brother's beloved Tamar—
one first and then the other one.
I was the new life in his old clothes
not undersized but differently
proportioned. Another treaty made
with scarcity, this, where I have
his widow and am obliged to make
nephew-sons, continuing his line.

She has no gift for silent suffering—
My theories are becoming known.
The priests accost me on my way
and riddle me dread warnings in
a parody of tact: What poison
can it be that when expended
properly continues life
and yet will kill if wrongly drawn?
I have no venom for my wife;
I say that poison is in point
of view, proportion, place, and all
but wheat, within a wheatfield's bounds
are weeds, and the more that is not wheat
the worse.

8

I say to Judah I
am poisoned with the seedy increase,
the chanted lists of names to lengthen,
the generations declining down
from Adam, and me, *Aleph* to myself
at least, and final *Tav*, too, a clot
within the blood of our connections.

In Chezib's bazaar at age fourteen
a sleek Egyptian healing man
spoke to me as he milked a snake.
The first principle of poison
in harvesting or healing is
to draw it out. He grasped the shaft
behind the head's blunted angles
gaping the mouth to press the fangs
into the goatskin cap of a jar.
The slow drops sliding down the sides
collecting in the bottom with
the light, measured the long moments
of my concentration. Grinning, he told
about a snake that spits its venom
nine paces: blameless natural image
and guilty conscience of the race.

One heat may weigh impartially
on everyone and each may have
his remedy. I heal myself
of all the automatic feelings.
A few great clutches and it's over.
Purged of desire then, I emerge
to see things as they really are.
I do not want a woman now
although I sometimes think of them.
There's nothing for the tribe in this.
I am talking to myself.

Samuel

I don't remember if it was before
or afterwards that I was told the story
of Samuel and Eli and God's summoning.
It doesn't matter since I know it now.
But I was five or six then, no more,
and having tamed the darkness of my room,
I balanced on that certain edge of sleep
which reconciles and reunites the worlds
of things and thoughts, when several times,
and clearly, in a voice I didn't know,
someone said my name. And terrified
I ran away into my mother's room.

Often my thoughts go back to this, the children:
first Samuel—three times mistaking God's voice
for a teacher's, calmly giving God,
the fourth time, words that Eli taught to him;
then me in my untutored horror, running.
Looking across the years again, I wonder,
although it must seem foolish, if it was
a kind of test, and something in myself,
then at my purest—stubborn and afraid—
refused the summons, denied the voice,
which would reduce the world to perfect sense.

Thomas called Didymus

And why should not one of my sort be sainted?
Hard-headed in an age over-credulous—
three false messiahs in those last four years—
among brethren who were either acquainted
so well with the performance of the miraculous
they never blinked at water to wine or Lazarus
redivivus, or otherwise, by turns, so hysterical
that everything He did was proclaimed miracle.
What followed was, in His words, (and did appear)
a God-forsaken agony, death made flesh
at least. How not require a simple test?

Of eleven only I was made to wait
the promised third day and another eight.
Not singled out for visions of empty tomb
and angels, but rather for a lone exclusion.
He knew my chief temptation: to return,
the twin of many, to versions of myself
of old, wanting things truly to seem
as ordinary as they once had been.
My faith was much like miracle itself:
rational nature in utter overturn,
His fingers probing always in my wound.

A left-handed man wrote this

Arched over, a retrospective swan,
my fist and wrist and arm do more than shadow
cross the page, they shade it, going back on

what I write and smearing. You would never know
to read this crisp, square immovable type
the wrong slant that I have on things, the low blow

fate dealt, how left is victim of the right,
how my own mother made into an error
the way I held my spoon, how father would fight

to force my throw, how saxophones and scissors
opposed or were altered individually
as orthopaedic shoes. O had I been a fencer

then those who looked in mirrors just to see
themselves had better have found one to imagine
like me, advantaged by unfamiliarity.

If only we wrote as Hebrew still is written,
in what clear track would come from my pen the code
for sounds! If only my name weren't Benjamin.

JOINING THE STORY

My Ancient Fathers

My ancient fathers
in Schecem and Jerusalem
took grave affront at a mere
tug upon the ringlets of the dark
patriarchal beard,
and the accidental hands
that brushed the Lord's high ark
were a dead man's.

My grandfathers in the ghettoes
of Munkacs, Vilna and Prague,
suffered not the razor's touch
upon the temple side-locks,
and as a sign upon their arm,
tight against the skin,
they wrapped the leather thong
of tefillin.

My fathers in the towns
of Belsen and Dachau
with shorn heads burned
in shame—and still they teach
what they have learned:
to take the altars in
out of the world, beyond the reach
of men.

Lifting the stone

Not when I call them do the pictures come:
I intend to sleep, and a landscape I never knew
I noted reels by as if seen from a car—
tufted grass backed by a stand of trees,
or a cityscape of grey apartment houses
remembered for no reason that I know of,
not backdrop for events, just incidental
music played between the acts, a scene
to watch as scenes change, till a blurry image
of a wooden shack in New York state somewhere,
equally random seeming at first, clarifies
as one of the oddly assorted places
my father pointed out for its resemblance
to the hut that he was born in.
                              I'm nowhere then,
abstracting his story out of its settings,
wanting to think of it as a large stone,
a boulder under which are things I need.
The straw-roofed Czech village, and the camps
with the strung wire through which the dark eyes plead
like droning whole notes on a musical staff,
a diagram of sorrow, are a stone
which I, a Theseus, putting off majority,
can't lift.
            And even imagining I can
takes the forms of my anxious dreaming.
I struggle from room to room in some cold warren
and the class has moved, or *Zeyde*'s deathbed
is in thirty-*four*, a stern attendant says
as if I should know. So these are the Chinese boxes.
The shrinking gift sequentially deferred,
the expectant rise defeated over and over
by another box. The earth conceals its bulk
until the stone is dug out, hugged up,
and below the stone is another, and under that

again a stone, on down into rooty dirt.
Inside the hole I have not properly pictured
in my mind but which in logic must be there,
I finally come to sword and sandals but
they are tiny—baby shoes, a toy sword.

Joining the story

The child's lateness was not yet resistance
to adult demands. He had merely forgotten
time and would be reminded by the hands
of his father who waited, so deep in his own story
of terror and loss that even the angry beating
of his heart was fear. When he saw the boy he joined

the ends of his belt in his hand and rushed to join
his child down the street before resistance
on either part. The child did not see the beating
coming, and if he saw it, he has since forgotten
his father's face then. The setting of his story
was lower: his father's legs, belt, whirling hands

between parked cars, his own warding hands
out of his picture of black curbs, sidewalk-joins,
one glimpse perhaps of a girl in the second storey—
people all over the night and no resistance
in the warm air to the sounds of what's been forgotten
long since, some talk, a radio, a quick beating—

minor, and nothing like the beatings
the father got. One of them at the hands
of a young soldier may not be soon forgotten
because he will tell his son, and it will join
those things that are passed on about resistance.
The father struck the soldier in the story.

The man kept spitting in his food. That story
happened in a labor camp, and the beating
was severe, with no chance for more resistance
in a room where they had sticks in their hands,
the first soldier and the others who joined in.
Not killing him, though—perhaps they had not forgotten

some small thing yet, in all they had forgotten.
Later, he'll want the father to recall the story
of his little beating though how can the son enjoin
him to? He cannot say on this date my beating
happened—you frightened your son with your hands
and your belt. He knows his father's resistance

to memory. His father has forgotten that beating
when his son, late, took the story from his hands,
joining it after the worst and without resistance.

The ballad of fighting with my father

My father and I would strive together
every evening just for fun;
more like a brother than a father
sometimes to his only son.
But father always by restraint:
he died at gunfights round the couch,
and never would forget to faint
to end our rolling wrestling bouts.

He changed our duels with weaponry,
a gift of swords of lamp components,
assembled at the factory:
one his, and one for his opponent-
son—and they had the heft that made
things real, each bellguard truly tolled,
struck by the pipe that passed as blade,
and all that brass to me was gold.

I started waiting up for him
as if I nursed some ancient insult,
and nothing promised or forbidden
could make bedtime less difficult.
To keep peace he would have to fence,
arcing his own attack so slowly,
and overpraising my defense—
all purest choreography.

But always I quickened the pace,
deaf to anything he warned,
I would keep swinging for his face,
until I fell into his arms,
yielding only when exhausted.
And what I meant when I would aim,
and what the blows would do if landed,
I had no more idea than Cain.

Meyer Tsits and the children

In the gone world of Roman Vishniac's book
of photographs of Jewish Eastern Europe
which we sit down to look over,
my father recognizes for certain only
the village idiot of a Munkacs neighborhood,
Meyer "Tsits," whom they used to tease:
"your mother has breasts"
the children would say as they passed,
and frothing with rage he would give chase
some years before breasts and Meyer were ash.

In the picture, though, Meyer is
contentedly on his way to a meal at the home
of the prosperous burgher who walks beside him
wielding a cane and wearing a *shtreimel*.
(My father thinks the fur-hat means it must be *Shabbos*.)
Meyer's benefactor protects the sable tails
from the drizzle with a draped handkerchief
and performing his mitzvah, taking
an unfortunate home to dinner,
he looks more foolish than the fool.

Even in the still one can tell how Meyer moves
on rain-glossed Masarykova,
hands tucked into opposite sleeves
making a muff, shuffling the spancelled
steps of a Chinese woman
when Vishniac sights him,
transfers his photographer's gaze down through
the viewfinder of the hidden reflex camera
held at his solar plexus
and out through the lens which peers through
the gap in his overcoat.
In the direction of the background,
straight back until the stacks of firewood,

up stairs behind wrought iron,
through the tiled entry,
rooms burst with Rabbinovitz's court
where Hassidim argue passionately
over matters of indifference
to those outside their picture
of the world to come, the messiah,
and the immortality of the soul.

Out of the book open on a table
in the dining room of this house,
I extend the scale of the photograph
into the world—
and my father's cellar rooms
in 1937 would be somewhere
in the schoolyard of this suburban
New York neighborhood.
But my father would not yet have been there.
Even at the late hour of the photograph
aged fifteen he welded in Fisher's Bike shop
on Kertvarosh which crosses a few blocks
from where Meyer walks,
and my grandmother Yeta Feige
still launders clothes in someone's basement.

Vishniac clicks his shutter.
Meyer is caught especially unaware,
after and before—no children near to show him
stripped to his Oedipal machinery,
though here in this moment, as in his rage
or his final agony, he was incapable of other modes than candor.

Meyer himself would have survived no selection.
He would have been among the first,
as in 1939 they practised Holocaust
on his sort just to get the knack.
The picture has been hidden, captured,

liberated, restored while other negatives perished
in the journey from their moments.

My father, who has come through much to get here
prepares to turn the page.
His own escape and liberation
may not be on his mind now.
There are so many losses and Meyer is little to him,
so few survivals and a picture something but not enough.
The dearest faces to him from then
are faces not in this book,
faces of which there are no extant images
outside of memory.

Meyer Tsits and the children
may not signify to him that before the astounding
cruelties are the ordinary ones,
which have been restored to us at least—
the cruelties of sons and fathers,
cruelties which may be partially redeemed
by forgiveness and therefore for which
forgiveness is seldom sought,
cruelties not on a street which lead to streets
which lead to the camps
where Meyer still and always in his first
childhood, in his first love and jealousy
was first for the gas.

I delay with questions the turning of the page.
What does the sign behind them—Mydlow—mean? How old was Meyer?
And it comes to me suddenly that I want
my father to ask forgiveness of Meyer Tsits
for peasant amusements,
for laughing the blank laugh
at those one thinks one never will become,
and that I must ask, too, for having made
some part of his life and death

into coin, capital for speculation.
And to ask forgiveness of Meyer Tsits is to
imagine him restored to faculties
he may never have had,
and to believe for a photographic instant
in the immortality of the soul.

The breaking of the glass

He observed that the rabbis present were very gay.
So he seized a costly goblet...and broke it
before them. Thus he made them somber.
                                        Talmud

Make me a wedding glass of crystal
to outlast the shrillest pitches
of a solid scream,
the heel above the temple
and the people dragged
along the shards.

One true form of tears
is heaps of glass—
from windows with their faces kicked-in
and the family's crystal
and all the unlucky mirrors of the houses
now with their several million faces
that cannot reflect.

God gave Moses a mouth
that brimmed with glass
that when he spoke
his pain was keen
and the blood came to his face.
This was His way of saying:
I am the Lord
my voice is in
the gusting of the wind
and the stuttering of men
and the breaking of the glass.

Not when you call them do the pictures come

In all of his alarm at the late departure
he still had his American thought for the day—
that he might be the only one in Ireland
at that moment who was concerned with time.
He retains the look of what he was doing:
fumbling the keys to the floor, slapping a book
under his arm—considering the lighted radio,
whether it needed extinguishing.
                                    Sometimes he left
it on for hours, a tree falling in the forest
and no one to hear. It might have been playing,
as it often did in his presence, great works
by the masters kept at bay in the background,
spending their largesse almost out of range,
but now it was saying a small country's news.
As he turned away to objects demanding sequence—
the bunched rug in the entry, the door, the lock—

the sounds at the verge of consciousness
became words as the ticking seems in motion toward us
in the dark bedroom, swelling into notice.
Perhaps it was just the syntax leaving till last
that the eight year old boy injured in the car
accident on the Naas Road, County Dublin,
in which his father had been killed, the child who was
expected to survive had died that day

which brought it in on him so, in past the simple
machine of his attention. So that he hardly
knew he had heard until he began to cry
for that son, and sat down to be late
for the class he was going to teach, feeling foolish
and yet instructed all over again, by force
as it seems he must be, in what he might have known.

In dreams the memory of dreams

I have something to say that I will say here
for want of a better place to say it.
Though I wrote in another connection
"I am a loving scientist of these regions"
I am no scientist and have conducted
no survey or experiment
in keeping with the method of science,
assuming what I have discovered
is available to such methods.
All I have is a sampling of one
and conviction, a certainty,
that when I dream and only then
within a dream I have memories
of other dreams I do not have when I'm awake.

Once, a poor statistic,
and on this occasion
a species of exception
which supports the rule,
I looked for and found details
of a dream I jotted over tables
for metric conversion and definitions
of rood and perch in the back of
a notebook chiefly kept
for other things and which I had forgotten
until I dreamt quite another dream
apparently unrelated to the first.

But still, in the second dream in which,
though this is possibly without importance,
I am backing-up a car disadvantaged
by a rear-view mirror of the sort
that makes things small
and in the car are my father
and my American uncle—
my mother's brother; I have only one other

uncle on my father's side,
a tailor and a remnant left us from what the Germans
Hungarians and Ukranians cut.
There are some logs I am in danger of backing
onto but I refuse all help from passengers.

In the midst of the reversing
I am remembering the earlier dream in which
a friend and I happen on a flooded plain
which we must move along but do not
have to cross. There may be some connection
implicit in ideas of conveyance,
or lack of it, since in dreams
absence may so strongly refer
to what precisely isn't there,
but between the convex mirror
and watery landscape is the link I think.

At any rate, beyond this single,
partly-documented case, I know
this happens to me frequently,
and though I am only one person,
I am the only one that I can know
in this way and feel I do know
by me that the phenomenon exists

with all its implications
that that dreaming side
refers to itself also,
remembers and connects
those conglomerate
events that take place in it.

I only know myself in this regard
as I say, but I must feel that I am not alone
in this. How can I be?
Although I've wished it otherwise
I've taken commonality for proof

that they must need as I do,
that I will heal as they have.
Resembling other people,
I must resemble them
in the memory of dreams while dreaming.
The poem is my only forum,
if you know of anyone who can
verify this occurrence,
who knows anyone who makes similar claims,
or better still has it happen to her
or him please say so, speak up,
let me, let someone know.

The castration of Abelard

He who is wounded in the stones or has
his member cut off shall not enter the
congregation of the Lord.
                    Deuteronomy 23.1

What fearful
conviction it must take
to castrate someone. Certainty
must flow in the bright blood
like some disease—
like syphilis, potential,
ready to flourish as much
as twenty years later.

I do not mean the act
itself, this is for hire—madmen,
perverts, drones—
but the consignment.

The matter seems mistakenly
clear now to some. A cleric
must not do
what you did, but for your marriage
they might have had your
benefice, but not
your tonsure. And God's
justice is neither
poetic nor jocular.

It was, whatever the disguise,
bloodlust to
bind you like Gloucester
to a chair and blind you
of children.

You say it involved
little pain, you did not

even want to
kill them later,
still the pain

was endless: to fatten
like a capon or a choirboy,
to be made docile, a lobotomized
victim of another's madness,
to be forcibly evicted
from your sense memory, which,
dim as it always is,
must be renewed to be recalled,
not to be what you were
ever again, to have no more
hair than a woman,
not to be a man,
not to be a woman either.

After the punishment

After the punishment,
a stiff-necked
few came down
out of the hills
and up out of cells
and of these none
could have deserved
their lives.

Among them later,
and their children
likewise, some lit candles
and did the 613 other
things
with conviction.
Others did some of these,
a few did none.
Some found,
for remembrance,
the punishment
was enough.

POSTURES

Postures

What their configured bodies said—
in a makeshift room, a borrowed bed—
a mattress wedged along four walls
like dustpaper lining drawers
in that pantry given for their nights
(her room-mates recognition of
their true and intramural love).
When they were in they were in bed

where shedding shadow more than light
a candle stood among the cans,
and Chinese wind-chimes hung becalmed,
a minor echo of the color
flagging at the candle's end.
They were among each other's arms
at rest, when neither told the other,
afraid to be analysand.

But when he profiled at her breasts
she was all woman and his mother.
Such fishy thoughts will flash from depths
and disappear. He turned things over,
unsettled though. Then on his chest
she lay as if a listener
and heard he was all men to her,
father, configured bodies said.

Upright in a car

Have you ever found yourself upright,
sitting in a car, telling the truth?
Abstracted by the seeming infinite
geometry of the indeterminate points
of this straightest of practicable real lines,
the highway; points without final definition,
being neither departure nor destination.

Each passing present position is no place
to you then, sealed in speed—gone before
it can be considered, like now which is over
before it can be pronounced to be now.

The road rushes to the prow and landscapes
glide by unclaimed—and towns and other lives
and towns and other cars. The bull's-eyes
marked on maps are no target of yours,
are their names on signs or constellated lights
after dark, themselves skirted now.

Only the coming mountains, if there is vista,
may be viewed as they move in from the distance.
Of the lovely roadside tree, a flash. The birch,
itself in a fog of other trees perhaps,
or merely the night highway coming on
within the limits of the headlights,
and the peripheral tick-by of fence, and hypnotic
drone or dash-dash-dash of the white line.

And you have cave-feelings under the closed
car's close ceiling, marooned with a companion
on the island of journey, at no risk
for telling it, or feeling at no risk.

Is it that journey and the idea of journey
resonate together, that you draw together

with another and yourself? There is where
you are going, and in some midway of the journey,
there dispenses with its childish fractions—
half-way, three-quarters, almost—and assumes
its significance, arbitrary and clear,
and seems then a judgment deferred indefinitely.

And you are, your voice is, a kind of stillness
in the midst of motion, like meditation defined,
or enacted in a metaphor.
                              Looking at the world
through glass, the road straightens after cant,
the signs continue their assurances
about direction, the great arteries of road
branch on and you open your heart, clearing things
as if you were writing them, things coming as clearly
and slowly as if you had written them before,
but slowly for it is just coming to you, yet clearly
as if you had set it all down before, as if
what you are writing has no need of revision.

Walking in the dark

Walking in the dark I crouch,
speaking braille with my sleepwalker arms.
For ceilings come down, and passages narrow
and extend. Burrowing the long dark,
body-hair becomes sensor, antennae
again. Doorposts brush past
the body, excepting suddenly
head, or

shouldered through to another room,
the arms and legs of chairs
clutch and kick, dislodged books
flap away from shelves, from the table
sharp corners point out soft parts,
and mirrors reflect absence
from the walls.
                    Passing through,
a cold beam of air
marks nowhere like a spotlight.

Walking in the dark fears heights.
Down on the floor a tack
flips over on its back like a turtle
in a show of helplessness, straight pins
stand up like blades of grass,
coils of electric wire
are garottes for the ankle,
and the vengeance of the outcast
shoe waits in the footpath.

There would be no up or down
in outer space, dead-reckoning
by the blue flame of the gas pilot
lights, distant as stars in the kitchen,

transcend the terraced cliff of the stairway,
inviting departure.

Listen, the metronome clock ticks
time—2/4 allegro—and the tap
drips it. Walking in the dark I crouch,
not to make a smaller target,
but retracting, in and in
towards my dark center,
for camouflage.

The parable of don't look

He demanded that the dark continue,
but even curtains pulled and shade
let light leak through
so he barricaded:

turned tables up against the window,
tacked blankets to the frame,
but they sagged and billowed,
and still light came

oozing through the cracks he'd tried
to staunch with rags until instead,
bandaging his eyes,
he wound his head.

In memoriam Professor Samuel Konefsky

Rising before dawn sometime to note down a dream,
leaning across the margin of the bed in darkness,
I try to read space with my fingers so the light
would find untangled lines, and when I came to see
I might then read and maybe understand
myself through image and association.

Instead I think of you, Sam, the association
simple enough I suppose. Abandoning the dream,
it is your presence I think to understand,
and how you managed a scholar's work in this darkness.
Paper caged behind guide-rails, I seem to see
a machine for aligning the pen to write without light—

as a nightself scrawling for its daylight
amanuensis? No, my own association.
You used a braille-typewriter and the phrase "I see,"
ordinarily, but did so only in dreams.
Struck down by a coach as a child, you woke to darkness
and later the aching work it was to understand

America's constitution and to understand
better than nearly any. The way you anchored you light
table napkin, this page, a clearing now in darkness,
angle diamond-wise into association.
Tucked in your shirt, pendant, I did not dream
it was method: childish even to a child to see

a man do. I didn't know then; we would see
you only at your home. I came to understand
looking through your books in my usual dream.
"Who reads braille?" I piped, my voice alight
to show my knowledge, making no association
between your eyes' saccade and darkness.

When you answered I ran into the darkness
of another room, ostrich-fashion, afraid to see
how I had hurt your feelings, my own association
with misfortune so slight I couldn't understand
that you were used to it. Now full, the light
whitens the paper a moment in which I dream

I understand how we are dilettantes of darkness
who see to return. From each of yours you send light,
laden as a word dreamed with our best associations.

Coal

Often and oftenest at night we would
run out of coal, and with the seven of us
in the house and someone always sick, there was
a need to keep the fires up high against
the vigilant damp of Irish winter.
Coal was my chore. I so loved fire it was
a sort of family joke to wonder that
I managed not to roast myself with all
my tending. But I didn't love the night.
Determined, I would take the tallest scuttle
and set out for the shed as for a journey—
hardly far-off enough behind the house.
it was, to notice stars between the roofs.

I propped the door to let the houselight in,
and shadow layered onto shadow, dark
grading finally down to the black coal pile
along the wall. Fumbling for the shovel
on my knees, I watched my moon-luminous hands
phase-out, extinguished by coal dust and dark.
At last I found the handle and relief.
The first shovel loads resounded on
the bucket bottom like huge hailstones pounding
a tin shed roof, and then the sound went duller.
I made the shovel fly, ramming and scooping
thick chunks of night until they bounced
around me and I turned to see the flat
black oval of the scuttle's mouth transformed:
heaped-up into a contoured silhouette.
Two-handed I would lug away its iron weight.

Grass patches bearded with a frosty down
were slippery and the ground uneven,
so rushing back into the house I let
my motion top the scuttle off. Tomorrow,
tomorrow there would be again behind

the house a trail of holes in the bright morning
for me to gather up and take away,
like shattered pieces of the night I feared.

Once safe inside I played the proud provider,
but not before, almost against my will,
just through the door I had to pause and stare,
confronted by the hearth, perhaps half-stunned
by light, to contemplate this glad paradox,
this miracle of burning rock.

A late exchange

One leans in at the door-jamb,
in undershirt and jeans, barefooted
on his way back from the toilet.
The other is a centaur: man
from the waist up; below bed—
covered in a hairy blanket.

For several hours he's been offended.
The argument he now resumes
they have as yet not had aloud
concerning what his leaning friend said—
at Carol's party—on his childhood,
Would the leaner step into the room?

Did he recall the joke about...?
(I was that friend. I won't say what
it was now; then I'd need reminders.)
"A joke nobody understood
but you," I said, "and such a minor—"
"Let me decide if it's minor or not."

Shivering, I retrieved your shirt
from the floor, night seasonably cold.
"I thought you had a sense of humor,"
I struggled for reason's baritone.
"Your sort of kidding often hurts."
The injury was singing tenor.

I looked down, busy doing buttons.
Your shirt constricted across my chest,
"Look," I began, "I didn't mean..."
stopped to think, "did I?" when you asked
if I'd just promise not to let on—
"What's this," I snapped, *Hamlet*?: 'Swear, swear!

Never make known what you have seen.'"
I grabbed your turtle-neck from the chair,
dove in—and tangled, head swallowed
in some wrong turn of sweater, breathing
through a mask of wool I suddenly found
what was no sooner found than followed

to its end—a spoor, the traces leading
me instinctive as a hound,
from and to this moment where,
thrashing upward toward the light
I ducked to make you disappear,
smoke reprised the bar, curry the house

where unfortunate remarks were made,
until peculiarly some scent
reminding me of you despite
your presence I pulled through in stages
to: dragging my scalp, nose, mouth—and out
to face you there, to promise then.

Van Gogh's Boots

"When I got home I was so angry that I threw the poor plaster casts in the coal bin, and they broke in pieces. And I thought: I will draw from casts only when there are no more hands and feet of living beings to draw from. I then said to Mauve: 'Man, do not speak to me again about plaster for I cannot stand it.'

*

Theo, I am decidedly not a landscape painter; when I shall make landscapes there will always be something of the figure in them."

Van Gogh, Letters

I

My old, still-serviceable shoes have moved me deeply,
angled in conference toe to toe, looking as self-opposed
as one could wish of an emblem of the common life,
till I resolved that they must sit for me and I moved them:

setting them side by side like brother boats anchored down by a quay.
Yet for surface I surround them only with the murky green
of undersea, as in the focus of an excluding mind.
For untied they drift away, trailing their lines,
one pair of which eddies into a sickle, a question
even in the stillness as the left one floats,
of whether the right may founder, half-furled in the uppers
and sloped badly by the rough weather of my rolling gait,
as if I always walked one foot in the furrow one on the crest.

Often on the plowed Dutch ground, they are splashes of black
like the browny black below, before, the green to be brown
to be gold to be bread of a wheatfield under sun or crows,
under the small and separate maelstroms
of each star's swirling fingerprints.

II

Cast of, cast off me
life-mask, shed skin
I will put on again,

every ridge, headland,
seam, footprinted—
so much mine

they are mine no longer
but the boots
of the Borinage miners

with whom I tried
evangelizing,
tongue-tied to the gospel

still I saw their shoes.
Later, their feverish skin
I mopped in fever.

*

Lolling tongues, at least
eight sets of blank eyes,
the sole you cannot see,

wearing through, and the heel:
because we live here, too
we call these places

after ourselves and ourselves
after these places.
They in the Borinage

live in the hollows
of their faces
and as if the land

held them in its cupped palm,
and Old Man Piet on a bare hill
in winter like the head

of an old man with a tonsure of frost
and the cloudy eyes
of two small ponds

and on either end
of his clenched fist
is a winter tree, bare and forked.

*

The dark clothes of the world
I can bear better just now
than its shining body.

Submission kneels
in the sagging knee
of my britches in a pool

of themselves just out of the picture,
fallen from the back
of a rush-bottomed chair.

But these boots are resistance,
chafing me to change
and changing with me.

The hilly upswell,
the rocky bone's bulb,
I roof with a little light:

granting a small triumph.
For I know that what we clothe
is the urge to nakedness

which presses up toward freedom,
and these also
are forms made of the struggle.

Victoria

To relinquish mourning without forgetting the dead
may require a difficult balance. Where many people
keep a memento of the dead, others resort to...mummi-
fication, with rooms and clothes left undisturbed as if
the dead were still there or might yet return, as
Victoria left the Prince Consort's rooms.
                                                D.W. Harding

Reader, for months I left the rooms just as
they were: the disposition of a household guard
of military bristles, paired Lancaster
rifles, and the eight point garter star.
But nothing sentinel enough to bar
what's come to pass, so from its bedside casket
I kept in order his watch's tattoo: Pass,
Friend Time. But the clothes' soft scattered discards
withal, since that fourteenth of December,
provided wakenings with evidence
for which to wake again: my eye, dissembler,
sleepily trailed his things, his precedence
seemed early rising only, sweet instants
forgetting even that I must remember.

The sleeper

Calming now in the dark to which he wakened
with a start, determining the shouts
of distress from the street were instead a tone
softly recurrent in the breathing out
of the sleeper at his side, he starts again
at having forgotten he was not alone.

Nocturne: knowing who it is

Only half heard and through the bedroom door,
the rustling bedclothes might be taken for
rain's sudden brush across the night outside.
The voice he'd know anywhere. That odd sigh,
hers surely. Still he leaves his desk to see
how what she murmurs in long gusts can mean
nothing to him—how she, delirious,
looks not distracted now but serious,
attentive elsewhere.
                          He stands thinking the poem
he works on has her left in their bed alone,
the poem that disturbs sleep and wife,
but he can know these moments of her life
with it that she can't know herself, asleep,
even moments that she fell asleep,
as, loving, he knows angles of her body,
even in mirrors she could never see.

Between us

Between you, who say too little,
and me, who says too much,
there is no one, none for the golden middle,
no one in the room but us.

Wedding photographs

You seemed to like to have your picture taken.
At first I thought it was that you were vain,
though I know better now. You had taken
such care posing for the flash, but all in vain,

for when the pictures came I had to smile
the way the camera so much caught you
flinching, or stranded solemn between smile
and smile. So I begin to see that you

must know the way, looking at them now,
if not to be more easy in your life
than I, then braver. We are married now,
and teaching me will take a life.

Passing, and suddenly in the mirror just then

Suddenly, passing in the mirror then,
that face, it was your face looked out of mine.
Quickly gone, I could not do it again:
the angle or the light, no no the line

the mouth made. Shaken, hazy, all at once
I *know*, thinking, "evidence. That's why—love—
some dim narcissism. But no it's since
isn't it? Your face in mine because of."

In single beds

In single beds what we have shared
is a fate, not just a bed, paired
like spoons inside a tranquil drawer

in one small bed so many times,
as waves bump other waves to shore,
you touch me and your dreams touch mine.

Somewhere in you, on a troubled scree
a rolling few sleep-stones of yours
have changed to avalanche in me,

and we have awakened once or twice,
huddled in the sweats of nights'
individual nightmare
and discovered it was shared.

The switch

With me out cold on the downstairs floor
after a comradely drunken night,
You had a thought that was almost pure.

Trying more fully to enter my life,
to feel what I feel being me,
you crept upstairs to try my wife

in both desire and curiosity,
and what else was there do you think?
Trusting mistaken identity

to dark and sleep, and dream and drink;
to bless the enterprise with success—
broad Comedy's spirited wink.

You moved across the room, undressed,
into a final act for farce,
when she aroused by your caress,

cooling my ardor with a curse,
turned you an unreceptive arse.

The lover she married

It occurred to her that he
might have performed
this act in just this way
with someone else.
His vocabulary in love,
to which she'd added something,
as finite as another's:

habitual turns of phrase,
and accent fixed enough,
so that what coinages
there were, new flair,
might stand out clear and please,
those times that she would not—
as now she did—suspect
his latest eloquence
had been informed
by others' current usage.

But she was wrong.
Despite persistencies
of act and actor,
the point of leading many lives
for him was that each was
another one, a time

that he might try to be
in metaphor at least
so free a variation
on what he'd been elsewhere,
at other times,
that it might almost make
him someone else.

Lachrymal

Though I cried plenty,
I never saw a tear-duct
until I was twenty.

Searching for a stye,
I came upon it
in someone else's eye—

startled when I did,
because I thought it
a wound in the eyelid.

Later, she wept a lot
on my account,
but I never forgot

it was not in a mirror
that I discovered first
that peculiar hurt,
the source of a river.

The numbered set of human faces

The numbered set
of human faces
is hardly infinite.
I have been to places
startled to have met

beloved dead—
an instant in the eyes,
the well-known head
or quick look recognized,
that strangers had.

And you my dear
rancorous friends,
your simple faces will appear
where you have never been
as comfort to a traveller.

For my daughter, concerning beauty

There are still people living who
will fall for statues—
from Aphrodite, punishment
for insufficient
self-love, that we imagine
warm animation
possible in those unmoved

others whose
noble foreheads clearly ought
to house high thought,
whose bright eyes seem made to speak.
Love what's complete
without you, for a time, my daughter—
you hate after.

Next year

Next year's invisible leaves
have shed old skins. Southwest of here
the diamondback and harlequin sleeves
of snakes, already twice this year
have snagged rocks, logs, and low things,
as snakes, frictional, purposeful,
as cats, escape old coverings—
moving against the ground like muscle.

Through the chrysalis' burst back: wings—
are these the things that are not made
to happen. Trees surround with rings
another year. The skin's scars fade.
There is nothing you can prefer,
take these as signs. There are few others.

ALL ANGELS ASK

But what is spontaneously brought forth by the people is often preserved only by the form impressed on it by the feeling and thought of the poet, or by the speculation of the learned. Also Jewish legends have rarely been transmitted in their original shape.

Louis Ginzberg, *The Legends of the Jews*

Israel

I have wrestled Jacob's angel,
all night, nor did prevail.
It was not principle we wrangled,
but each minute detail.

His headlock early placed within,
I could not throw him off.
He touched a sinew of my sin,
to alter how I walk.

Departing when the morning came,
even though I failed,
he smiled and gave me Jacob's name
and called me Israel.

Names

Great-great grandmother bore an angel.
Miraculous nativities for Jews
were common then. We made of our sons
so-called angels so Czars could not. We called
midwives discreetly, made no record of birth,
these children sheltered in among the names:

Itzhak ben Zvi, Avram ben. . . Hebrew names
confused the Czar's conscriptors, death's angels
who kidnapped boys twelve years from birth
for thirty years in armies where a Jew
was forbidden to be a Jew except in cat-calls.

                    *

My great grandfather was Nathan, Nathan son

of Jacob, who, in turn, was Jacob son
of another Nathan, as still we keep the names
of our loved dead for children, so to recall,
and name none Gabriel or for any angel,
fearing, we cautious Ashkenazic Jews,
such names would tempt the hosts to prepare a berth

in heaven.
                    *

          Great-grandmother sickened after child-birth.
Days past the circumcision of her son,
according to the custom of the Jews,

at synagogue, though absent, she was renamed
Chaya—meaning life—to confound the angel
of death, who might with luck still call

at the old address. Till she mended, all called
her Chaya—who had been Lena Konefsky at birth,
for by her father's time there were no angels,
and every son was only *someone* son
of *someone* in the shul. Now there were names
by which officialdom enumerated Jews,

male and female, for harvest, since the Jews
had been made to take surnames or be called
something from a list, sometimes ungainly names:
Rosebush, Mountain Rock, mark such rebirth.

                    *

My mother's father stood before one son
of Ireland, uniformed, therefore no angel,

who joked with this Jew unfresh from a sea-berth,
and called him in the book, not Koppelson,
but Kopp, a name for striving with angels.

All angels ask is a little courtesy

All angels ask is a little courtesy,
coming in disguise,
they want to be
treated like one of the guys
seldom is. All angels ask is a little courtesy
and Sarah delivered. A cup of tea
though they don't need it,
and some wine,
a good feed—it
reminds.

Then to business. A belly laugh
and a belly for Sarah courtesy of Abe
who got himself some unexpected sap
in eldest age.
A miracle or two
(all in a day's work) Lot's rescue
or another birth:
The Lord Is Pleased To Announce The Coming Here On Earth...

All angels ask is a little hospitality
and they take it kind of personally.
Used to be
they'd turn a trick or two, a never-ending porridge bowl, three
wishes or a bang-up exit
after kindness,
so you'd know who it was, and later
(keeping an eye
out for a guy)
on in life, in time of need, a favor.

These days they skip the exit and you'd never have known the need
fulfilled was for a good deed
done a fellow stranger but for a dumb
mundane do-gooder glow
that they supplied at source. They still come

if this is what you need to know,
the rules are a little tighter now:
no tricks, no sleight of cosmos, and since the flood or Sodom
or something, no brimstone flattening for punishment. They still come
though,
if this is what you need to know

everything is still seen, made note of, just things have gotten more
          serious
in the universe,
perhaps heaven, being no longer sure
that hell is not an empire or is more
than it once was, is watching
(all angels need is a little love)
and biding
the time it has so much of.

They still come, though.
If this is what you need to know
the person sitting next to you could be
an angel and all angels ask is a little mercy.
Every single U.F.O.
is the sighting of an angel—if this is what you need to know
all angels ask is a little humanity
never mind
heaven and hell
all angels ask is a little lovingkind-
ness, and you can never never tell.

The passionate exegete to his love

Man before his birth, being pure spirit, knows everything; but at the moment he sees the light of day, an angel strikes him on the mouth and he forgets the whole Torah.

Ludwig Blau

*

Between morning and evening the angel carries the soul around, and shows her where she will live and where she will die...and he takes her through the whole world, and points out the just and the sinners and all things.

Louis Ginzberg

That every mark upon the soul is made
upon the body, I know and I can prove,
if you allow your mouth and mine persuade.
My people say—above the lips, that groove's
an angel's, who taught our souls before the earth
all we would know here. Then his finger left
us dumbstruck and disremembering for birth,
and living to recall what we again forget.
Note how instinctively the finger fits
that space still when it's silence we request,
the soul's soft clay mnemonic on the lips.
So if I seek your silenced lip's impress
to match with mine, it's that I wish to wake
a memory of heaven, and for knowledge's sake.

*

Heaven, lips, soul! A practical poem made
to win you. We can all the pleasures prove
is what I mean to say, mouths persuade
indeed. The needle's wearing out the groove
in my head where you're recorded. Remember-earth
we-come-to-in-the-end is suasion better left,
with young girls, alone, strictly. You're the birth
of the blues in thirtyish me, singing forget

69

it, rightly maybe, except I feel it fits—
your fawn coloring leggily makes requests
of its own, and sweet downturn of your lips
natural refusal. Who'd not impress
you with love songs, sonnets, anything to wake
beside you? Girl, give in for heaven's sake!

*

The Rabbinic version of the tale is made
less for etiology than to prove
knowledge determinate, and to persuade,
too, that it's heaven sent. The charming groove
in your lips aside, presumably the earth-
bound, carnal knowing I infer is left
a place in lore, not just allied with birth,
elsewhere. The knowledge we're lip-struck to forget
is word-bound. The efficacious word fits
behind all this. *Let there be light* requests
the world to make itself by word of lips,
as by words the angel's teaching must impress.
But by fingers we're dumb, by mouth's breath clay wakes
to words which would be breath again for our sake.

Sons of Adam

It's certain Abel didn't live to breed,
while Cain wed one of those new women sprung
from nowhere. God's tattoo on him intrigued
her. So, bad-boy allure and *born to run*
assured his seed's continuance till Flood.
Then all aboard the ark were all God left,
and Noah's clan came from that later brood
of Eve and Adam, blank unstoried Seth—
from whom, then, us. His entry in the Bible,
obituarial: begotten, he begot;
named to replace his herder brother Abel;
departed aged nine-hundred; survived by Enosh.
A born forbear for us, no great repute
of either sort, sent in as substitute.

Colloq

We are like some fantastically unlikely fairy tale
told to keep the children of the world
deceived to the order of things
the fish swallows the amnesiac long-lost lover's ring
as it rolls off the bridge into the water and
the fish is caught and cut open by a cook
and the cook finds the ring
and wears it in the street
where he is jumped and beaten severely by a gang
of hoodlums who take the ring
and one of them recognizes it as his very own Esmeralda's
and locates her fortunately by the name and address written
on the inside (unnoticed by both cook and amnesiac) since the ring
was once a dog tag
so Esmeralda is found and the hunchback mugger marries her
goes straight and gets a job at a local church
or maybe you are the ashes of a paper ballerina
and I am a charred lump of tin a little lighter than the
ordinary tin soldier because I was unfortunately crippled
(short a limb) due to a war-time lack of tin
we are destroyed but together and me in the shape of a heart
to sort of symbolize that somebody or something somewhere affirmed
our great love even after you returned to ashes and I to tin
which is o.k. really since I would have destroyed you in bed
or maybe more like the story of the little girl
who got confirmed in theses red shoes
and she couldn't stop dancing
even at the funeral of the old lady that adopted her and this
angel said she would dance until she was a skeleton
so she waltzed over to the executioner who fitted her with
some raw red stumps which hampered her dancing career
and eventually she was saved
which made a whole lot of sense since she was just a kid
and she didn't know red shoes weren't standard operating procedure
for confirmations and/or funerals

and who the hell cares that she was so happy
that her heart broke and she died and
went straight to the head knock who took her in and everything is
          supposed
to seem just fine to this little kid that you read it to
before bed time except for the dancing red stumps that will keep him
          good
and God who loves him
meanwhile I was always the little tailor who got seven at one blow
or maybe six ninety eight if things got tough
but somehow I always got to stepping on Thumbelina and feeling bad
about it afterwards even though it was clearly her fault for getting under-
foot and you were Snow White fine and fair with a penchant for apples
and my kiss was always better than a bromo
and we would always live happily ever after in twin beds
under cover of vows and I would at least die for you
(as it turns out I will get hit at an intersection by a moving van
but nobody will collect since the light facing him was out
and the whole regrettable incident would not have happened
if I were a few inches shorter since as it was the damn thing only
lobotomized the tip top of my head
which did the job anyway)

Old cars, my ancient cars, where are they now?

The lion-hearted, soft-blocked Studebaker
whose model shared its name with small birds, and sipped
such quantities of oil I had to buy
oil used, too, centrifuged—recycled truly,
still took me from New York to America
before gaining a place in landscape's still-life,
a version of the bleaching steer-skull
somewhere in Nevada's roadside desert.
Out to discover the Pacific for myself,
I travelled under mission-like duress,
and so I cast away the number plates
and cannily filed the engine block free
of serials, a ditching with implied
apotheosis—who could confirm the death
by numeral or know the resting places,
each one unfinal? Any flattened stratum
in the badlands at the edge of every city
might be merely, junked or dumped, the carcass
before the come-back as part of a Cadillac,
or twists of steel reinforcing concrete,
or skyscrapers' molded angle-parts.

My transport lay in stalling such translations
in cars about my age. Each jury-rig,
ardor invented: muffler-trusses done
in baling wire, a vacuum cleaner pipe
prosthesis for a severed tail-piece,
chewing-gum stanched the radiator's drool.
Sills sagged; doors shut just for initiates
(a lift and pull at once and not too hard).
Million dollar fifty dollar cars
reprieved from the boneyard by visits to it
for transplants from less fortunate relations.
Each journey would exhaust the driver's will
in constant prayer that things might hold together.

Bilateral zoomorphs of mine: "Buick
Super" with sharky grin and little fins
in whose front seat I first contrived to sex,
permitted only by degree—each of
her sought parts a battle for a beachhead;
V.W., simian upper lip in front,
thoroughly monkeyed with, my first wept-over
vivisection, vitals boxed for months,
wrapped up in pages of how-to manuals.

And some I must record as mine which were
mine only in the way one owns what one
habitually observes. My childhood Hudson,
all dorsal curve, belonged to Mr. Goodwin—
even to lean on was forbidden—he kept
look out from his window—a "Wasp" deluxe,
four door—a pair of neighborhood singletons
in '53. The Schwartzs' beat-up Nash,
always parked in the space beside the corner,
was a "Rambler." "Vagabonds," and "Nomads," "Way-
farers," lived settled lives around our streets.

Such given names enciphering childlike desires
of adults—for speed, rank, and several kinds
of flight, passed children by as self-referring.
For most of us, an "Eldorado" seen
downtown was El Dorado more than myth.
Amelia Earhart named the "Terraplane"
which promised land what aero- and hydro- gave
to their respective elements already;
the first delivery went to Orville Wright;
a codger told me at the auto show.
The Wrights I knew by then from school, same book
but later chapters than "Patrician" or
"Imperial." "Earhart, Amelia" I looked up
and learned that asking where she might be now
is more and less rhetorical than usual.

But with my family, by our Ford, through travels
upstate in the summer, I was brought
Time's mysteries first hand—something called
a "Reo" rotting in a field in Monroe,
New York, and gangstery Hupmobiles twice
come upon in barns near Pottersville.
I loved the small escutcheons, hood-effigies,
gap-toothed chrome letters nearly spelling out
gone names then sighted here and there now cited
here in a verse: Crosley, Graham, Cord,
and Willys, Kaiser-Frazier, Cunningham.
One last Mohican Packard I did have
later, the adjustable suspension dropped
body on wheels irrevocably one day,
and one once-ordinary Plymouth six,
a forty-seven bought in seventy four,
old-womaned along to church for years,
the head so carbon-crusted from scant use
the engine blew, and heartless I sold the body.

Uncustomized, unsouped-up, remarkable
for a mild longevity when I got them,
and marked by past lives. Not just the scars—
someone's misprision in back-up or turn,
but decor's minor illegalities:
the knob for one-hand whirling 360 turns,
bolted to the steering wheel, the dashboard's knick-knack
Jesus, the classic soiled sponge dice suspended
from the mirror—all I left intact out of
respect for characters too set to change.

How well I can remember. How do I
remember? Long past student days and salad,
the truth is I left them only lately and only
for a time perhaps, surely the last of all
with whom I rode and rattled—whither now
my lost companions is another story.

But I have seen in earthly visions in
exotic places, full-voiced as ever,
calling and growling, schools, shoals, herds,
in tight and mixed formations—forties Chevvies,
fifties Fords, De Sotos, Pontiacs,
smoking blackly in the streets of Damascus,
Mexico City, Lima, La Paz, Seoul
(and all old conquests and dependencies);
chained round with yellow checks taxiing
through Istambul; stolen, smuggled, of value,
in Port Au Prince. They let the clocks go round
and round or disconnect them, poor men with deft
small hands who keep these things alive forever.

Notes

Beyond illuminating points drawn from Jewish culture that may not be in general currency, the notes that follow have more to do with origins than explanations, with the corollary more than the necessary. Many are comments I have found myself making when reading in front of an audience that I don't have to imagine.

AMNESIA. One way students of movement—actors, mimes—are taught to think of a clown is to imagine total innocence, a creature without history or precedent applying himself to the objects of the world for the very first time.

DAVID. The persona is a sort of contemporary David voyeuristically observing his Bath-sheba-figure. Among the things I have added to this version of the story in 2 Samuel 11 is the heat-wave. *Hamsin* is the middle-eastern equivalent of the Californian Santa Anna gales, carrying not only high temperatures, but also a saturation of positive ions in the air which seems to contribute to its sinister effects on human behavior. In Islamic law *hamsin* may be offered in mitigation for the defense in cases of violent crime, which dramatically increase at these times. The poem occurs during a lull in the wind.

My original intention for the phrase "goes to ground" was the hunting usage describing the behavior of an animal returning to the burrow.

The closing lines are not biblical quotation, but the gist of King David's commands concerning Bath-sheba and her husband, Uriah.

SAMSON. This poem filters Samson's active biblical persona through a more amplified interest in language. Samson was consecrated to God by his mother, who had been barren until God, answering her prayers, gave her Samson. She in turn gave back Samson by bringing him to the High Priest. The riddles and events belong to Judges 14-17, but the voice sounds very much like that of an "unacknowledged legislator" addressing the philistines he knows.

ONAN. The poem's first line incorporates the opening of the Hebrew Prayer "Mah Tovu": "How goodly are thy tents O Jacob, thy dwelling places O Israel." I elaborate the persona of this Onan out of the brief account in Genesis 38. Onan's brother Er was "displeasing to the Lord, and the Lord took his life." Onan was then compelled by his father Judah to make a "levirate" marriage with Er's widow in order to "provide offspring" for his brother. Onan avoided his duty: "But Onan, knowing that the seed would not count as his, let it go to waste whenever he joined with his brother's wife." What the Bible describes as wasting seed or spoiling it on the ground is now generally acknowledged to be "coitus interruptus." In the poem, I

78

trade on the older interpretation, also enshrined in the word "onanism," of masturbation. *Aleph* is the first letter of the Hebrew alphabet, *tav* the last.

SAMUEL. The story of Samuel and Eli and God's summoning can be found in 1 Samuel 3. Samuel lived with the Priest Eli. Like Samson he was the answer to a barren but pious woman's prayer. He therefore was also "dedicated" to the Lord soon after his birth.

THOMAS CALLED DIDYMUS. Didymus means the twin in Greek. The details for this piece, spoken by Doubting Thomas, come from John 20, a part of the Christian Bible that seems particularly full of lovely touches, human and quirky. Mary Magdalene is the first to see the empty tomb and later the angels. Excitedly, she comes to Peter and John (who refers to himself as the disciple whom Jesus loved) with her news, touching off a foot-race for the sepulchre between the two which John wins. Jesus finally reveals himself to Thomas, providing the requisite proof of resurrection. Thomas then states his belief in Jesus' divinity. Jesus' response, to my ear, drips with Jewish intonation: "Blessed are those who have not seen and yet have believed."

A LEFT-HANDED MAN WROTE THIS. This persona comments on the fictional business of speaking through a mask. While there is, naturally, no way to tell whether or not the writer is left-handed, the reader knows the writer's name is not Benjamin, which means in Hebrew son of the right hand. (The writer is a righty, was a fencer, and has only observed the trials of left-handed friends).

MY ANCIENT FATHERS. Stanza one refers to Uzzah who, on the way to Jerusalem, saves the ark of the covenant from falling off a cart when an ox stumbles, and dies immediately upon touching it (2 Samuel 6).

The three cities mentioned in the second stanza were all important Jewish centers. Munkacs (or Mukachevo) has special significance for me as the area from which my father comes.

The earlocks, or *payehs*, are worn at the temples by Hassidic Jews. *Tefillin* are phylacteries, Jewish ritual objects with leather thongs and boxes. One set is worn on the head, the box part placed on the forehead; the other is bound around the arm, with the box on the upper arm near the shoulder. These boxes contain four biblical verses which refer to the commemorative acts of binding and placing signs. Line thirteen echoes a phrase from those verses.

LIFTING THE STONE. *Zeyde* is Yiddish for grandfather. Theseus, left with his mother, comes of age in the myth when he is able to lift the stone his father has placed over his birthright: the hero-sword and the sandals.

MEYER TSITS AND THE CHILDREN. The photograph, taken on a Munkacs street in 1937, is number 123 of Roman Vishniac's book, *A Vanished World*. Vishniac says that he concealed his camera for these pictures, but he does not specify the kind of camera or the style of concealment. *Tsits* is Yiddish for tits. *Shabbos* is the Jewish Sabbath which begins at sundown on Friday.

THE BALLAD OF FIGHTING WITH MY FATHER. Abel was the first death; there was no human precedent. This and the textual difficulty in Genesis 4.8 allow for some ambiguity on the question of Cain's premeditation. When he "set upon his brother, " what could he have expected to result besides a venting of rage?

THE BREAKING OF THE GLASS. The epigraph from the Talmud (Berakhot 31 a.) refers to the origin for the Jewish custom of stamping on a glass at the conclusion of a wedding. The breaking of the glass is a reminder of the destruction of the temple in Jerusalem. The Talmud contains many anecdotes cited for the purposes of explanation. Some are extra-biblical tales used for biblical exegesis. According to one such legend, accounting for Moses' stutter, the Pharaoh's advisors designed a test to indicate whether the baby Moses would usurp the Egyptian throne. The infant Moses must choose between cups: in one a jewel, representing power, in the other a glowing coal. At the critical moment, an angel guides the baby's hand from jewel to coal, which the child puts in his mouth. As a result of his burnt palate, he becomes a stutterer, but is allowed to remain in the palace. This poem offers the glass of Kristallnacht as another explanation for the stutter. Kristallnacht, "the night of glass," November 9-10, 1938, inaugurated a new phase in the movement toward Holocaust with pogrom. Glass flowed in the streets as Nazi violence against Jewish places and people began in earnest.

THE CASTRATION OF ABELARD. Heloise and Abelard are perhaps the most famous Medieval lovers. He, one of the finest minds of his age, a professor at the University of Paris, fell in love with the brilliant young woman whom he had been engaged to tutor. As a woman, Heloise's opportunities for higher education were limited. Together, according to D.H. Lawrence in *Lady Chatterly's Lover*, "in their year of love he and Heloise had passed through all the stages and refinements of passion." *Heloise and Abelard* by Etienne Gilson provides an extremely lucid interpretation of the story and clarifies some of the ambiguities and complexities of Abelard's position in canon law with regard to questions of celibacy and marriage. Abelard's castration was connived by Heloise's uncle and guardian, Fulbert, as a quite unofficial act of vengeance. After Abelard's calamity, his enemies sought to exclude his participation in religious orders with the biblical laws against priestly physical impairment.

80

AFTER THE PUNISHMENT. Traditionally, there are 613 positive commandments in the Bible. This number and what it represents are also commemorated in the number of fringes on a *tallit*, or prayer-shawl.

POSTURES. Body-position figures in the occasion of this poem, and of many that follow in this section. Giving rise to a revelation of a spiritual or emotional sort, posture takes on yogic connotations, while also recalling such synonyms as stance, attitude, or pose.

College apartments of the sixties seemed always to have brass-plated wind-chimes in the shape of Chinese characters.

IN MEMORIAM PROFESSOR SAMUEL KONEFSKY. My great-uncle Samuel Konefsky was professor of Constitutional law at Brooklyn College. He was an important scholar, a memorable teacher, and an extraordinarily sweet man. A Guggenheim fellow, he also spent a year at the Institute for Advanced Studies at Princeton. He authored *Chief Justice Stone and The Supreme Court*, *The Legacy of Holmes and Brandeis: A Study in the Influence of Ideas*, and *John Marshall and Alexander Hamilton: Architects of the American Constitution*.

Saccade (line 30) is defined in the *Concise Oxford Dictionary* as "brief rapid movement of the eye between fixation points."

COAL. The speaker, an emigrant perhaps, recalls his Irish childhood.

VAN GOGH'S BOOTS. "Two Shoes" is F 255 in B.J. De La Faille's 1928 *Catalog Raisonne*, and dated 1886. The painting—also entitled "Boots with Laces" in the reproduction I own from the Rijksmuseum—is one of a series painted during Van Gogh's time living with his brother Theo in Paris.

Since writing the poem, I discovered that Heidegger uses the boots, too, in an essay on the "thingly aspect" of the art-object which parallels some of my interests in this poem. Section one concludes with references to several other well-known paintings of Van Gogh. Section two alludes to the time Van Gogh spent as an evangelist among the miners of the Borinage region of Belgium.

VICTORIA. The epigraph comes from the *Times Literary Supplement*, "The Process of Mourning," July 4, 1980. Since writing the poem, I was excited to come upon the Queen's journal entry of December 14, 1878: "This terrible day come round again. When I woke in the morning was not for a moment aware of all our terrible anxiety, and then it all burst upon me." The anniversary of Prince Albert's death she refers to in this entry was also by a sad coincidence the day she lost a grandchild. I took pains that the objects associated with Albert in the poem were authentically his so that Victoria's thoughts might be hers, and I felt rewarded, that imagination's hypothesis had been uniquely proved. *Queen Victoria in Her Letters and Journals,* edited by Christopher Hibbert (Penguin's "Lives and Letters" series, 1985) also records her delighted completion of *Jane Eyre* on 23 November 1880, the final chapter of which begins, "Reader, I married him."

LACHRYMAL. The title can be adjectival—of tears—or a noun referring to an actual object, a little vessel for holding tears.

ISRAEL. Jacob wrestles with the angel in Genesis 32.25-33. The match results in a new name for him ("for you have striven with beings divine and human and have prevailed") and an injury to his thigh muscle that leaves him limping.

NAMES. In 1827 Russian Jews between the ages of 12 and 27 were made subject to draft. The government set high quotas which communities were responsible for filling themselves. Frequently, it was easiest to have the *khapers* (kidnappers, in Yiddish) collect boys from the poorest homes. The children, despite the law, were frequently under the age of twelve. Many died en route to the "cantonments," barracks where Russian soldiers abused them into submission to baptism. These conditions obtained in varying degrees of intensity until 1856. In addition to counting on lack of records and confusion in names Jews also were often forced to cripple children or blind them in an eye to avoid impressment and the concomitant estrangement from family and religion.

Shul, from the German for school, is another word for synagogue, rooted in its role as a place of study as well as prayer.

The shortening or other alteration of names was a feature of Ellis Island, and entry to the United States.

ALL ANGELS ASK IS A LITTLE COURTESY. Three angels come in human disguise to Sarah and Abraham, and receiving hospitality, they announce that the withered couple will produce a child. Sarah reacts with laughter, and her child's name, Isaac, comes from the Hebrew word for laughter. Two of the angels go on to Sodom where Lot shows them hospitality and the behavior of the townspeople confirms Sodom's wickedness. The angels destroy Sodom and Gomorrah but spare Lot (Genesis 18-19).

The ever-refilling bowl is a fairy-tale motif, a reward for having dealt courteously with fairies or other magical creatures.

THE PASSIONATE EXEGETE TO HIS LOVE. The speaker may be conceived of as the Jewish equivalent of a "spoilt priest." He is trained in scriptural exegesis. The platonic nature of knowledge assumed by the legend of the instructing angel evidences Hellenistic influences on Jewish thought. The vertical groove above our upper lip is called a philtrum (a word which also denotes a love-potion). The Blau epigraph is from the "Angelology" entry in the old *Jewish Encyclopedia*. The Ginzberg quotation is from his famous compendium, *The Legends of the Jews*.

SONS OF ADAM. God set Cain's mark on him, here conceived of as a gang-style tattoo, in order to prevent others from killing him—as Abel's murderer. Who those others might be, or where the wife Cain marries in Genesis 4.17 comes from, the Bible does not make clear. Eve says of Seth in Genesis 4.25, "'God has provided me with another offspring in place of Abel.'" The title translates literally a Hebrew phrase meaning human beings.

COLLOQ. The title is short for both colloquial and colloquy. The principal motifs come from Anderson fairy tales "The Steadfast Tin Soldier" and "The Red Shoes." Bromo Seltzer was an effervescent stomach remedy.

OLD CARS, MY ANCIENT CARS, WHERE ARE THEY NOW? Automobiles do populate a childhood in the United States. The immortality of these American imperial objects, which I myself witnessed in some of the far-flung places mentioned in the poem, now seems increasingly to belong to Japanese cars, judging by news footage. With the exception of the Volkswagen (VW), all the makes and models alluded to are American cars, from the thirties through the sixties.

All biblical quotations are from the 1962 Jewish Publication Society translation of the Torah, used with permission.